PRO WRESTLING LEGENDS

Steve Austin
The Story of the Wrestler They Call "Stone Cold"

Bill Goldberg

Bret Hart
The Story of the Wrestler They Call "The Hitman"

The Story of the Wrestler
They Call "Hollywood" Hulk Hogan

Randy Savage
The Story of the Wrestler They Call "Macho Man"

The Story of the Wrestler They Call "Sting"

The Story of the Wrestler They Call "The Undertaker"

Jesse Ventura
The Story of the Wrestler They Call "The Body"

CHELSEA HOUSE PUBLISHERS

The Story of the Wrestler They Call "The Undertaker"

Dan Ross

Chelsea House Publishers
Philadelphia

Produced by Choptank Syndicate, Inc.

Editor and Picture Researcher: Mary Hull
Design and Production: Lisa Hochstein

CHELSEA HOUSE PUBLISHERS

Editor in Chief: Stephen Reginald
Managing Editor: James D. Gallagher
Production Manager: Pamela Loos
Art Director: Sara Davis
Director of Photography: Judy L. Hasday
Senior Production Editor: LeeAnne Gelletly
Cover Illustrator: Keith Trego

Cover Photos: Sports Action
                Jeff Eisenberg Sports Photography
                All-Star Sports

The Chelsea House World Wide Web site
address is http://www.chelseahouse.com

First Printing

1 3 5 7 9 8 6 4 2

Library of Congress Cataloging-in-Publication Data
Applied for
ISBN 0-7910-5407-1 (hc) 0-7910-5553-1 (pb)

Ross, Dan.
    The story of the wrestler they call "the Undertaker" / Dan Ross.
        p. cm. -- (Pro wrestling legends)
    Includes bibliographical references (p.) and index.
    Summary: A biography of Mark Callaway, the mysterious profes-
        sional wrestler known as the Undertaker.
    ISBN 0-7910-5407-1 -- ISBN 0-7910-5553-1 (pbk.)
    1. Undertaker (Wrestler) Juvenile literature. 2. Wrestlers -- United
States -- Biography -- Juvenile literature. [1. Undertaker (Wrestler)
2. Wrestlers.] I. Title. II Series.
GV1196.U54R67   1999
796.812'092--dc21
    [B]   99-38098
                                                     CIP

Contents

1 A WEEK IS A LIFETIME

D ark. Mysterious. Intimidating. "The Undertaker" emerged from the shadows to stalk his World Wrestling Federation (WWF) foes for more than a year. Now he was Hulk Hogan's problem: a 6' 9", 329-pound ghoulish nightmare with a ghostly gaze that sent chills down his opponents' spines and made them feel as if they had been touched by something . . . otherworldly.

Who was he? Where did he come from?

On the surface, the answers to those questions were simple. He used to call himself "Mean" Mark Callous. He came from World Championship Wrestling (WCW). But since arriving in the WWF in mid-1990 and billing himself as The Undertaker, his frightening aura had made everyone forget what he once was, because he certainly wasn't Mark Callous anymore.

He billed himself as being from "parts unknown." Many people suspected he came from another world, a place closer to the afterlife than this life. When The Undertaker stepped into the ring, a dark, sinister cloud hung over the WWF. There was something disturbing and unusual about this man, something his opponents didn't want to confront. He was deliberate. Dangerous. Deadly. The question wasn't, "Who is he?" The question was, "What is he?"

In 1990, when The Undertaker first appeared in the WWF, his rule-breaking ways and ghostly demeanor cast a dark shadow over the federation and threatened three-time WWF World heavyweight champion Hulk Hogan.

Teddy Long was "Mean" Mark Callous's first manager in WCW. He let Mark take the place of injured tag team wrestler Sid Vicious on the Skyscrapers, but kicked Mark off the team once Vicious recovered.

Well, he was not a patient man, not by any stretch of the imagination. And he was tired of being dismissed by people like Teddy Long, his first manager in WCW, who bumped him from the tag team the Skyscrapers and replaced him with the wrestler Sid Vicious. He was tired of people like Brother Love, the manager who brought him to the WWF, and shortly afterward sold his contract to another manager, Paul Bearer.

Perhaps it was true: people simply didn't want to deal with him. Paul Bearer, though, was perfect for the job. Paul Bearer—as in pallbearer, a person who carries the coffin at a funeral. In this case, it was Bearer's job to carry The Undertaker's urn, which according to the myth that quickly developed around this mysterious monster, contained his mystical powers.

He would need them all on this night.

It was November 27, 1991, the night before Thanksgiving. The event was the Survivor Series pay-per-view at Joe Louis Arena in Detroit, Michigan. The Undertaker's opponent in the main event was Hulk Hogan, one of the greatest WWF World champions of all time.

During a fabulous career that already included three WWF World heavyweight championships—including one reign that lasted four years—Hogan had overcome his greatest challengers, from King Kong Bundy and Randy Savage to Andre the Giant, Ric Flair, John Studd, and Kamala the Ugandan Giant. The

"Hulkster" had faced athletes, he had faced beasts, he had faced opponents most men feared, and he had beaten them all, even the seemingly unbeatable.

In The Undertaker, Hogan faced a challenger who had plowed a path of destruction through the WWF. The Undertaker's "tombstone" piledriver had become one of the most devastating finishing maneuvers in the world, capable of crippling its victim. The Undertaker would lift his opponent, turn him upside down, and bury him, jackhammer-style, headfirst into the canvas. Then, just for good measure, he might lock his opponent in a coffin, or bury him up to his neck in a mock cemetery plot.

The art of intimidation had never known such a master artisan as The Undertaker, who was a man of few words, but chillingly effective actions.

Yet, despite Undertaker's massive size and intimidating appearance, the experts were wholly in agreement that Hogan would survive this test, just as he had survived most of the others. Then the match started. Before long, this much was obvious: the experts were wrong.

The bout was shockingly one-sided. Undertaker neutralized Hogan with chokes and punches. Although Hogan was only 54 pounds lighter and one inch shorter than The Undertaker, he seemed tiny compared to this plodding giant. The Undertaker's massive forearms dwarfed Hogan's massive forearms. Even when Hogan pounded The Undertaker with punches and kicks, they had about the same effect as a young boy pounding against a brick wall.

The Undertaker tossed Hogan to the arena floor as if he were a rag doll, then choked him with a cable from the television equipment at ringside. The referee, a ring veteran named Dave Hebner, thought about disqualifying The Undertaker, but gave him time to release the hold. As a result, Hogan lost his only chance for salvation.

The Undertaker smothered Hogan for more than two minutes with a face claw. His massive hands, covered with the kind of heavy rubber gloves a coroner might wear, smothered Hogan's entire nose, mouth, and jaw, and threatened to squeeze the very life out of him. Hogan, a proud champion, managed to break free, but not before he had suffered unimaginable pain and suffering. When Hogan got up, The Undertaker grabbed him, turned him upside down, and delivered a powerful tombstone piledriver.

The match should have been over. The force of Hogan's head striking sickeningly against the hard mat rocked the building. The crowd watched in stunned silence, waiting for The Undertaker to cover the champion for the pin. But this time, it was The Undertaker who must have been wondering, "Is this man human?" because Hogan not only rose to his feet, but proceeded to batter the stunned challenger.

Suddenly, The Undertaker was in for the fight of his life. Hogan delivered a body slam, then went to the ropes for a legdrop, but Bearer reached out and grabbed Hogan's right leg. That's when Ric Flair, a former World champion and Hogan's fiercest rival, emerged from the locker room, walked to ringside, and grabbed the WWF World championship belt.

Hogan was incensed—and momentarily distracted—by Flair's appearance. He left the ring, slugged Flair, then returned to the ring and

Undertaker kneels in deference to the urn in his manager Paul Bearer's hands, for he says his mystical powers derive from the ashes stored within.

stunned The Undertaker with a boot to the face. Hogan prepared for another legdrop, but again Bearer reached out and grabbed his legs.

Hogan tried to grab Bearer. The referee got between them. The Undertaker smashed Hogan in the throat, then lifted him for another piledriver. As the referee argued with Bearer, Flair slid a folded metal chair into the ring. Undertaker ruthlessly piledrived Hogan onto the chair and covered him for the pin. Miraculously, the referee turned away from Bearer long enough to make the three-count.

It was as shocking a three-second turn of events as the sport had ever seen. An enormously popular champion had fallen. A feared rulebreaker had ascended to the top. Flair and Bearer were ecstatic, while The Undertaker even allowed himself a smile.

The Undertaker, in only his second year as a professional wrestler, had won one of the most prized championships in the entire wrestling world. Hogan didn't even realize what had hit him. Dazed from the impact of the final piledriver, he lay in the ring, then stumbled back to the locker room. Later, he had to be rushed to a nearby hospital.

The crowd at Joe Louis Arena couldn't believe what it had seen, or what referee Hebner hadn't seen. The WWF World championship had changed hands in the most incredible, and seemingly the most illegal, way possible.

Undertaker hoists an opponent and prepares to deliver his signature finishing move, the tombstone piledriver.

But The Undertaker's glory and the crowd's dismay would not last long.

Because of the controversial ending to the bout, WWF president Jack Tunney ordered a rematch six days later in San Antonio, Texas.

This time, The Undertaker wouldn't be so lucky.

In Texas on December 3, Flair's interference backfired. Bearer's interference backfired. The Undertaker had locked Hogan's arm behind his back and walked him toward the ropes, where Bearer prepared to bash Hogan with the urn. But Hogan ducked and Bearer mistakenly struck Undertaker. Hogan knocked Undertaker to the mat, scooped up the ashes that had spilled from the urn, threw them in The Undertaker's face, and covered him for the pin. The match lasted just over 13 minutes.

The Undertaker's title reign had lasted only five days. In almost the blink of an eye, The Undertaker's glory had turned to bitterness. The smile had been replaced by the familiar haunting glare. Once again, there was darkness. Once again there was mystery.

Before long, there would once again be intimidation.

The Undertaker, like any other challenger to a championship belt, knew the cold truth of wrestling: an eternity could pass before he'd get another chance at the title. Perhaps he'd never again be WWF World champion.

In less than a week, he had experienced enough glory and heartbreak to last a lifetime, and an afterlife.

2 THE MASTER OF PAIN

The mystery of The Undertaker deepens when one attempts to research his past. Where did he come from? Where was he born? Characteristically, he simply won't say. Even his WWF biography lists him as hailing from "parts unknown." Published biographies list him as having been born in Dallas, Texas; Death Valley, Arizona; and Las Vegas, Nevada. This much, though, is known: he was born on March 24, 1965, probably in one of those three places.

This much, too, is known: his real name, of course, isn't The Undertaker, it's Mark Callaway. He was an athlete who played football and basketball in college. He went on to play college basketball at a small school in Texas.

Very little else is known. It's as if The Undertaker purged his past to make it seem as if he really did come from . . . well, let's just call it the other side.

In 1988, at the age of 23, Mark Callaway reached a crossroads in his life. There were two things he was certain about. He knew he needed money, and he knew he could beat the professional wrestlers he had been watching on television. So he found a wrestling school in Texas, borrowed the $2,000 tuition from his brother, and began training to become a professional wrestler.

Before being incarnated as The Undertaker, Mark Callaway was known as "Mean" Mark Callous, "Master of Pain," "Texas Red," and "the Punisher." At 6' 9" and 320 pounds, he was a monstrous, hair-raising opponent no matter what name he used.

Mark Callaway first made a name for himself when he wrestled Jerry "the King" Lawler's USWA heavyweight title away from him in 1989. But Lawler (right), a veteran wrestler and former AWA World heavy- weight champion, won the title back from Mark just two weeks later.

After only two lessons, however, the school's instructors stopped showing up. Mark was enraged. He was out $2,000, and it wasn't even his own money. He spent the next year working as a bouncer in nightclubs so he could pay back his brother. Mark's dream of becoming a pro wrestler had dampened, but it hadn't died.

In 1989, Mark finally found a legitimate place to train, and he spent several months working hard: lifting weights, learning moves, and discovering the psychological aspects of being a professional wrestler. Finally, in early 1989, Mark made his pro debut in the Central Wrestling Alliance (CWA).

Not surprisingly, this 6' 9", 320-pound monster with the pale, expressionless face and long reddish-brown hair made quite a first impression. Opponents were immediately intimidated by this daunting figure who went by the name Master of Pain. And, unlike most big men who were strictly brawlers—kickers and punchers with few wrestling skills—Mark had some genuine aerial and mat skills to go along with his raw power.

As it turned out, finding a moniker that fit was one of his most difficult chores that first year. During 1989, he would be known as "Master of Pain," "Texas Red," and "the Punisher." Two of those names, the Master of Pain and the Punisher, were appropriate. From the start, he was a fierce competitor who pummeled his opponents. He pounded them with powerful fists and beefy forearms and floored them by smashing his muscular arms against their throats. Occasionally he threw in a dropkick that, given his considerable size, was always unexpected. When opponents looked into his eyes, they saw no mercy.

In no time at all, there were indications that Mark was destined to become a major star in the mat sport. On April 4, 1989, in Memphis, Tennessee, he defeated Jerry Lawler for the United States Wrestling Alliance (USWA) heavyweight title. This was a remarkable victory for Mark. Just a year earlier, the veteran Lawler had been the American Wrestling Association (AWA) World heavyweight champion. After only a few months as a pro, Mark had already defeated a former World champion, and a legendary one, at that!

But as Mark quickly discovered, an athlete's fortunes rarely go quite that smoothly for any real length of time. Just two weeks later in Memphis, he lost the title to Lawler.

Mark moved on to the Dallas section of the USWA, where again he defeated a former World champion. This time it was Kerry Von Erich, the former National Wrestling Alliance (NWA) World heavyweight champion, who held the USWA Texas title. Again, Mark's title reign didn't last long; Von Erich regained the belt shortly afterwards.

The impressiveness of Mark's debut, however, couldn't be denied. In less than six months as a rookie, he had defeated two former World champions for championship gold and done so in very impressive style. That's more than many established wrestlers accomplish in a lifetime!

It soon became clear, however, that Mark needed to do something to take his career to a new level. Suddenly, after competing against top stars and winning, he began losing to lesser wrestlers. As a result, he rarely received title shots. It was as if he was becoming a forgotten man.

That's when a major opportunity presented itself.

The NWA—which would soon be taken over by WCW—came calling with a contract. Mark wasted no time signing his name to the bottom line. He changed his name to "Mean" Mark Callous and made his debut as a rulebreaker, disliked by the fans and feared by opponents.

Then came what appeared to be his big break. Manager Teddy Long had formed an imposing tag team called the Skyscrapers, consisting of two of the biggest men in the sport: Dan Spivey and Sid Vicious. The Skyscrapers were involved in a brutal feud with the Road Warriors when, in early January, Vicious got hurt. Unwilling to sideline the team and desperate to settle his feud with the Warriors, Long turned to the biggest substitute he could find: Mark Callous.

Mark seized the opportunity. Long was criticized by the wrestling press for turning his back on Vicious, and Vicious silently stewed in anger, but the New Skyscrapers didn't lose a step. At the nationally televised Clash of the Champions X card on February 6, 1990, Spivey and Callous lost a battle, but won a war. The Road Warriors beat them by countout, but Callous and Spivey left Animal and Hawk lying on the mat and writhing in pain after Spivey attacked them with a steel chair. Two weeks later at the WrestleWar '90 pay-per-view event, however, Hawk pinned Spivey in a tag team match.

Soon after that loss, Mark discovered that loyalty wasn't a major characteristic of Long's personality. When Vicious finally recovered from his injury, Long booted Mark out of the Skyscrapers.

Mark was enraged. He silently feuded with Vicious and plotted revenge against Long. On April 6, 1990, in Atlanta, Long and Paul Ellering, another manager, met in a boxing match. Mark interfered, causing Long's disqualification and ending their relationship once and for all. Shortly afterward, Mark found

a new manager—Paul E. Dangerously.

As a singles wrestler, Mark fared well against opponents such as Johnny Ace, Brian Pillman, Tommy Rich, and Eddie Gilbert. Mark quickly moved up in the NWA ratings, and by the summer of 1990, he had moved into contention for the NWA U.S. heavyweight title.

By that time, Mark had added a heartpunch to his offensive arsenal and was developing the move that would one day be known as the tombstone piledriver. When the lineup of matches for the 1990 Great American Bash pay-per-view extrava-

Mark Callous got a chance at a title when he was matched against reigning NWA champion Lex Luger (above) at the 1990 Great American Bash pay-per-view. It was the biggest match of his career at that time, but Callous was unable to defeat Luger.

ganza was announced, Mark Callous was in the main event against U.S. champion Lex Luger.

But Luger—who, despite being three inches shorter and 55 pounds lighter than Mark—had held the belt for well over a year and was an imposing foe. In the biggest match of his career to date, Mark was pinned by Luger after getting floored by a thunderous clothesline, a stiff forearm across the throat.

Mark's NWA fortunes sagged after that loss. He kept losing to Pillman and lost another title try against Luger, this time by disqualification. On August 29 in Rome, Georgia, Mark suffered a devastating defeat to Junkyard Dog. Instead of moving up in the ratings, Mark was suddenly moving down.

At the time, Mark couldn't have known how fortunate he was when his NWA contract expired. He left the federation, lost a chance at the vacant USWA title, and then made two decisions that would change his life.

The first decision was easy. He signed with the WWF.

The second decision took a little creativity. Realizing he wasn't getting anywhere with the name "Mean" Mark Callous, he decided to change his name, his identity, and his persona. He would suggest to opponents and fans that he came from "the great beyond." He would enter the ring to eerie organ music and have his manager carry a golden cremation urn. A bell would toll when he appeared. If all went well, not only would opponents fear The Undertaker's imposing size and skills, they would also fear what he was . . . or what they imagined him to be.

His career about to be transformed, and the sport was about to be transformed, too.

3 | DAWN OF THE UNDERTAKER

A s the night of the WWF's fourth annual Survivor Series pay-per-view approached, one question was on everybody's mind.

Who would be the Million-Dollar Team's mystery wrestler in its match against the Dream Team?

Nobody knew. This much was certain: Bret Hart's Dream Team, consisting of himself, Dusty Rhodes, Koko B. Ware, and Jim Neidhart, would take on Ted DiBiase's Million-Dollar Team, consisting of DiBiase, the Honky Tonk Man, Greg Valentine, and a mystery partner in one of the four-on-four elimination matches at the card on November 22, 1990, in Hartford, Connecticut.

This much was certain, too: DiBiase's mystery guest would be an imposing person, not just a relatively meaningless fill-in wrestler chosen from the ranks of the mid-card competitors. DiBiase meant business, and he didn't like to lose.

The behind-the-scenes machinations started the week before the big event. When DiBiase found out that a 6' 8", 320-pound man named The Undertaker was coming to the WWF, he knew exactly who he wanted as his fourth man.

Even as the Survivor Series began, only a few people knew the identity of the mystery partner. When it came time for The

Following his debut in 1990, The Undertaker let the WWF know that he was a force to be reckoned with as he continued to triumph over wrestler after wrestler. The era of The Undertaker had begun.

Undertaker to make his ring entrance, organ music filled the air in the Hartford Civic Center. The house lights dimmed. The Undertaker stepped onto the runway and began his long, slow walk to the ring. Every eye in the arena was glued to this massive human being. He truly looked like a man who had come from the other side of the great beyond.

It was an impressive debut. The Undertaker needed only one minute and 39 seconds to pile-drive Koko B. Ware and score a pin. Throughout the match, he showed himself to be virtually impervious to pain. Dusty Rhodes, a former World champion, pounded on The Undertaker, who refused to budge. Hart's men double- and triple-teamed The Undertaker, but their collective efforts got them nowhere. With eight minutes and 26 seconds gone in the bout, The Undertaker rocked Rhodes with a flying axhandle (a double-fisted aerial maneuver that carries stunning impact), then scored the pin.

Unfortunately for The Undertaker—and for the Million-Dollar Team—the idea of beating up on a former World champion was too delicious a prospect for The Undertaker. Rather than turning his attention to the two remaining members of the Dream Team and trying to win the match, The Undertaker stepped outside the ring and continued his relentless assault on the defenseless Rhodes. Within a minute, he was disqualified.

But The Undertaker had achieved his purpose. He hadn't entered the Survivor Series to win it. After all, there were no titles on the line in this special match. He had entered the Survivor Series to make an impact and an impression, to make an entrance that people would never forget.

In a little over nine minutes, The Undertaker had told the rest of the WWF, "I'm a force to be reckoned with."

He seemed truly unstoppable. Two weeks later, at a WWF TV taping at the Sundome in Tampa, Florida, The Undertaker used his tombstone piledriver to win two matches on the same card. The next night, on the other side of the state, he flew off of the top rope and leveled Tugboat—one of the biggest wrestlers in the world—with a heartpunch.

The Undertaker's list of victims grew longer by the week: Dusty Rhodes, Koko B. Ware, Big Bossman, and Jimmy Snuka all fell prey to his deliberate fury and his tombstone piledriver. For the first time in his brief wrestling career, Mark Callaway was being noticed.

The impressive performances continued. Although The Undertaker didn't win the 1991

Looking like an undertaker himself, Paul Bearer carefully holds the urn that supposedly contains The Undertaker's mystical powers.

Royal Rumble—a battle royal in which wrestlers enter the ring one at a time and can be eliminated only when they're dumped over the top rope—he eliminated Bret Hart, Butch Miller, and former rival Kerry Von Erich. The combined forces of Animal and Hawk—two more old rivals—were necessary to eliminate him.

But not everything was progressing smoothly. On January 28, Undertaker's manager, Brother Love, was beaten up by the Ultimate Warrior and suffered an assortment of internal injuries. By that time, The Undertaker had already realized that Brother Love wasn't the type of management he needed to keep his career on the fast track.

Enter Paul Bearer, who eagerly purchased Undertaker's contract from Love. Like The Undertaker, Bearer had an alabaster complexion. He was strange and sinister, and he wholeheartedly embraced the spirit of The Undertaker.

Bearer would appear in interviews surrounded by caskets, smoke pots, and creepy green light. He took care of The Undertaker's urn, which he claimed was the source of his man's magical powers. Their favorite stunt was placing The Undertaker's battered victims into a body bag. Bearer and The Undertaker were a convincing duo.

Two days after he destroyed Jimmy Snuka at WrestleMania VII in Los Angeles, The Undertaker unleashed a heinous attack on the Ultimate Warrior. The Warrior wasn't just any wrestler. He was a muscular 280 pounds of pure popularity, and a former WWF World heavyweight champion. By ambushing the

Warrior, The Undertaker seemed to be asking for trouble.

The attack occurred during one of Bearer's televised interview segments, aptly named *The Funeral Parlor*. Bearer lured the Warrior to the set by promising him a gift. The gift turned out to be a casket embossed with the Warrior's logo. As the enraged Warrior manhandled Bearer, Undertaker charged to the rescue, knocked down the Warrior, stuffed him into the casket, locked the cover, and left him to suffocate.

Fortunately, WWF officials rushed to the set to rescue the Warrior, who had been desperately clawing inside the box for more than five minutes. This incident wasn't merely one of the scariest in WWF history—it was also an indication of how far The Undertaker was willing to go to destroy his opponents.

The Warrior immediately challenged The Undertaker to a series of "body bag" matches, in which the loser had to be carried back to the dressing room in a body bag. The feud was mostly one-sided. Although the Warrior scored a few victories by disqualification, The Undertaker was the one most frequently placing his opponent inside the body bag. He also buried Warrior up to his neck in a mock cemetery, scaring the daylights out of this previously fearless wrestler.

By September, the Warrior had left the WWF. Many people thought he had been frightened away by The Undertaker.

The Undertaker not only feuded with the Warrior, he humbled big men such as Kamala and Berzerker, and had his first confrontation with Sid Vicious, the man who had replaced him in the Skyscrapers one year earlier. The

After customizing a casket for Ultimate Warrior and unsuccessfully trying to bury him in it, The Undertaker became involved in a series of body-bag matches with the Warrior (above right), which Undertaker usually won.

Undertaker—not one to forget a slight—mercilessly choked Vicious—now known as Sid Justice—and rammed him into the casket. But this was not to be The Undertaker's night. Later in the match, Justice burst out of the casket, powerslammed The Undertaker to the mat, bashed him with the urn, and rolled him into the casket for the win.

It was a rare setback for The Undertaker, whose reputation was growing more impressive by the day.

Having risen through the WWF ranks, The Undertaker had set his sights on the biggest prize of all: the WWF World heavyweight title. Bearer petitioned WWF officials for matches against World champion Hulk Hogan. His requests weren't ignored, especially as Undertaker piled up victories over Big Bossman, Hacksaw Duggan, and Kerry Von Erich, all top contenders. His tombstone piledriver had become the most feared finisher in the federation. And he had proven his resilience. The Undertaker's trademark was to lie flat on his back after sustaining a beating and then, as Bearer raised the urn to the heavens, Undertaker would miraculously regain his energy, rise up, and destroy his stunned opponent.

Bearer and Undertaker got what they wanted. The World title shot against Hogan was granted for November 27, 1991, at the Survivor Series pay-per-view event. The Undertaker's dream was achieved that night in Detroit at the Joe Louis Arena. Thanks to some timely help from Ric Flair, The Undertaker defeated Hogan to capture the World title.

But the glory would not last. Almost immediately, WWF president Jack Tunney ordered a rematch to take place six days later in Austin, Texas. Hogan regained the belt, but the title was declared vacant because Hogan had thrown ashes from the urn into The Undertaker's face.

The title would be put up for grabs in the 30-man Royal Rumble on January 19, 1992, in Albany, New York. Glory eluded The Undertaker on that night, too. He was the 17th man eliminated as Flair, who had helped The Undertaker to title victory nearly two months earlier, won the World title.

And that's about when one of the most stunning reversals in wrestling history took place.

The Undertaker, the most feared rulebreaker in the land, was about to undergo an image change.

4 THE IMPORTANCE OF BEING URN-EST

The event that changed The Undertaker's career occurred on January 29, 1992, in Amarillo, Texas. Jake Roberts, who hated "Macho Man" Randy Savage, had decided to get even with Savage by attacking his wife, Elizabeth, with a chair. The Undertaker didn't take kindly to that at all.

Much to the surprise of everyone—especially Roberts, Elizabeth, and Savage—The Undertaker rescued Elizabeth from what could have been a brutal attack. The frighteningly violent Undertaker had carried out one of the most poetic deeds imaginable. He had rescued a damsel in distress from a violent brute.

Roberts couldn't believe what The Undertaker had done. Later, on Bearer's *Funeral Parlor* interview segment, Roberts confronted The Undertaker and demanded an answer to his question: "Whose side are you on?"

"Not yours," The Undertaker replied, his steely stare cutting through Roberts and chilling him to the bone.

The crowd went wild cheering for The Undertaker. In an instant, he had become a fan favorite without even changing the way he looked or the way he wrestled.

The Undertaker's action ignited a vicious feud with Roberts that culminated with a match on April 5, 1992, at

---

Each time The Undertaker was on the verge of pinning WWF World champion Bret Hart, one of Hart's friends would interfere to prevent The Undertaker from winning the title.

WrestleMania VIII in Indianapolis, Indiana. The Undertaker mercilessly piledrived Roberts on the arena floor not once, but twice. Undertaker won the match in under seven minutes, and the crowd loved every second of it.

Unfortunately for The Undertaker, his switch from rulebreaker to fan favorite was accompanied by a stale period in his wrestling career. Although he continued to win, his feuds and matches were virtually meaningless because they brought him no closer to contention for the WWF World title. He struggled against Sid Vicious. A long feud with Kamala, known as the Ugandan Giant because of his huge size, was one-sided in The Undertaker's favor because Kamala had a deathly fear of the coffin. Undertaker dominated Kamala in a series of casket matches and needed less than four minutes to beat him at SummerSlam '92.

The good news: The Undertaker never lost. The bad news: The Undertaker was getting lost in the WWF shuffle, overshadowed by Randy Savage, who had gone on to win the World title, Davey Boy Smith, who had won the Intercontinental title, and Bret Hart, whom Undertaker had beaten in a series of matches the previous fall.

This period of stagnation temporarily ended in September, when Flair beat Savage for the World title. The Undertaker received several shots at Flair, but the wiley veteran champion retained the belt simply by losing the matches by disqualification. In the WWF, a champion can lose his title only if he submits or is pinned.

With nothing better to do, The Undertaker started building a gigantic custom-made coffin in which he planned to bury Kamala. The

Undertaker finished the casket and finished the job at the 1992 Survivor Series by nailing Kamala in the casket.

It was impossible to ignore how little career progress The Undertaker had made in a year. At the 1991 Survivor Series, he had wrestled for the World title. At the 1992 Survivor Series, he had wrestled in a casket match.

Even so, the wins piled up. The Undertaker scored victory after victory over Razor Ramon and Yokozuna. Kamala's manager, Harvey Whippleman, posed a brief challenge to The Undertaker when he brought in Giant Gonzales, a 7' 6" monster with the stated intent of ridding the world of The Undertaker. At the 1993 Royal Rumble, Gonzales rushed to the ring and choke-slammed The Undertaker, starting a feud that did nothing for The Undertaker's career and lasted nearly eight months.

The war was interesting for close observers of the sport, though. The most intriguing aspect of the feud centered around the urn and its so-called mystical powers. During one match in Halifax, Nova Scotia, Gonzales attacked Bearer and stole the urn. For over a year, Bearer had claimed that The Undertaker derived a portion of his incredible strength from the urn. Sure enough, without the urn, Undertaker slumped. Desperate to regain his power, The Undertaker beat Gonzales and regained the urn at SummerSlam '93, thereby ending their feud.

Finally, in dramatic fashion, The Undertaker reentered the title picture. It happened when manager Jim Cornette stood in the ring with WWF World champion Yokozuna and claimed that nobody could beat the 589-pound former Sumo wrestler. Suddenly, the arena

In a scene right out of Beauty and the Beast, *The Undertaker revealed his gentle side when he charged to the rescue of the beautiful Miss Elizabeth, who was attacked by Jake Roberts at a January 29, 1992, WWF match in Amarillo Texas. Overnight, The Undertaker made one of the most difficult transitions in pro wrestling: from hated rule-breaker to fan favorite.*

lights went dark. When they came back on, The Undertaker was standing in front of the champion, claiming that he could beat Yokozuna.

Yokozuna, like Jake Roberts and Kamala before him, was terrified of The Undertaker and his caskets, but Yokozuma had plenty of friends on whom he could rely. He and The Undertaker clashed in the main event of the 1994 Royal Rumble, competing in a casket match for the WWF World title. Again, The Undertaker's flair for the dramatic stole the show and nearly ended his career.

Ten wrestlers helped Yokozuna stuff The Undertaker into the casket and close the lid. Green smoke emerged from the urn. The Undertaker, locked in the casket, was wheeled out of the arena and left to suffocate.

Suddenly, an image of The Undertaker appeared on the video screens in the arena. Speaking as if from beyond the grave, he vowed to get revenge on Yokozuna. Undertaker's image rose to the ceiling—magically—then disappeared.

This was one of the eeriest and most bizarre incidents anyone had ever seen. According to the WWF, The Undertaker had died and gone to heaven. Of course, that wasn't true. The Undertaker was alive and well. He did, however, disappear from the federation for several months.

He resurfaced on May 7, 1993, in Yokohama, Japan, but that singular match was followed by another long absence. Meanwhile, Ted DiBiase claimed to have lured The Undertaker back to the WWF with the promise of vast riches, and before long The Undertaker had returned.

Kamala the Ugandan Giant (left) and The Undertaker were involved in a series of casket matches, in which the victor would lock the loser in a coffin. Though the two wrestlers were matched in size, Kamala's deathly fear of coffins helped The Undertaker win.

Or had he?

One night, Bearer went face-to-face with DiBiase's Undertaker, who merely stared back at him. Was this the real Undertaker, or merely an impostor? Bearer was convinced that DiBiase's Undertaker wasn't the real deal.

Bearer was right. The real Undertaker resurfaced several weeks later with Bearer at his side and issued a challenge to DiBiase's impostor Undertaker. Their match at SummerSlam '94 was comically confusing. Which man was DiBiase's Undertaker? Which man was Bearer's

Diesel interfered during The Under- taker's match with WWF champion Bret Hart at the 1996 Royal Rumble, unleashing the wrath of The Undertaker, who vowed to exact his revenge. Later, while Diesel was wrestling Hart, The Undertaker tore his way up from under- neath the floor of the ring and pulled Diesel down into the hole.

Undertaker? Keeping track was nearly impossible, but when the match was over, the real Under- taker had put an end to the impostor with an easy pinfall victory. The fake Undertaker was never heard from again.

What followed in The Under- taker's career were more casket matches and more meaningless feuds. A serious eye injury side- lined him for several months. But he returned to the ring and got back on the title track when Bret Hart won the World title on November 19, 1995. While The Undertaker piled up victories by disqualification over Hart, Bearer demanded a series of no-disqual- ification title matches.

"It's been so long since my Undertaker had a title match," Bearer said, the frustration seeping into his voice. "I don't want outside forces to spoil his destiny."

Outside interference, though, did keep spoiling his destiny. Each time The Undertaker was on the verge of pinning Hart, somebody would interfere on the champion's behalf. On December 5, 1995, The Undertaker punished the champion for several minutes and prepared to execute his tombstone piledriver. Before he could execute the move, though, Davey Boy Smith, Yokozuna, and Owen Hart stormed the ring and got The Undertaker disqualified. At the 1996 Royal Rumble, on January 21, The Undertaker pinned Hart following a tombstone piledriver, but Diesel pulled referee Earl Hebner

out of the ring, resulting in Hart's disqualification.

Enraged by Diesel's interference, The Undertaker vowed to do everything in his power to
derail the man known as "Big Daddy Cool" and
prevent him from winning the World title. So
intent was Undertaker on stopping Diesel that
he interfered in a Diesel vs. Hart match by tear-
ing through the mat, rising through the middle
of the ring, grabbing Diesel, and pulling him
back under the ring! But where did it get
him? Nowhere. His reward was a match against
Diesel at WrestleMania XII, which sounded
great until Undertaker realized that meant he
wouldn't be wrestling for the World title.
Minutes after Undertaker won the match at
WrestleMania, two other wrestlers, Shawn
Michaels and Bret Hart, battled for wrestling's
biggest prize. Michaels won.

Then came two more feuds to nowhere,
first with Mankind, one of the most tenacious
brawlers in history, then with Goldust, the
cross-dressing son of "American Dream" Dusty
Rhodes.

It was the middle of 1996. Nearly five years
had passed since The Undertaker had won the
WWF World title. In that period, he had received
only a handful of title shots and had spent most
of his time settling grudges while his career
went nowhere.

When Bearer made one of the biggest mis-
takes of his life at the 1996 King of the Ring
pay-per-view event, the time was right and
the stage was set for another turning point in
The Undertaker's volatile career.

FALSE FRIEND

The battle between The Undertaker and Mankind was one of the most anticipated matches at the King of the Ring pay-per-view event on June 23, 1996, in Milwaukee, Wisconsin. The two men had been feuding since the day after WrestleMania XII when Mankind—a newcomer to the federation who previously had been known as Cactus Jack—fearlessly attacked The Undertaker. Mankind aligned himself with Goldust, another of Undertaker's enemies, and the two combined to play mind games with their new enemy.

If not The Undertaker's most formidable opponent, Mankind was certainly the most fearless. Mankind wasn't afraid of getting hurt. He certainly wasn't afraid of anything The Undertaker could do to him.

By the time Undertaker and Mankind met at the King of the Ring, each man was intent on ending the feud in his favor.

The match was a hard-fought brawl. But what people remember the most about the bout was what happened at the end.

With nearly 20 minutes gone, Mankind and Undertaker locked up in simultaneous chokeholds. Paul Bearer, clutching the urn, snuck up from behind, raised it over his head, and brought it down, apparently meaning to smash Mankind.

During the mid-1990s, as The Undertaker feuded with rival Mankind, he underwent a startling metamorphosis, first breaking with his manager Paul Bearer, then rising from the grave after a 1996 buried-alive match and going on to win a second World championship.

Instead, he smashed The Undertaker! Mankind applied his "mandible claw" maneuver, squeezing Undertaker's windpipe and rendering him unconscious, and won the match. When he recovered, The Undertaker couldn't believe what had happened. Either Bearer had made the worst mistake of his life, or he had intentionally caused Undertaker's defeat!

In front of the cameras, The Undertaker and Bearer acted as if nothing was wrong. Behind the scenes, though, they frequently argued. The trust between the two men had been tarnished.

When WWF president Gorilla Monsoon signed The Undertaker and Mankind for a match at SummerSlam '96 in August, Monsoon's goal was to end this violent feud. In fact, Monsoon added a strange stipulation. The match would start in the boiler room of Gund Arena in Cleveland, Ohio. The winner of the match would be the first person who made it from the boiler room to the ring and claimed the urn from Bearer, who would be standing in the ring. Mankind, who loved to brawl, especially outside the ring (he was a master of falls-count-anywhere matches), promised victory.

When the night arrived and the bell rang, The Undertaker and Mankind hooked up in a nasty brawl inside the boiler room. Undertaker got the best of the exchange and made it to the ring, where he prepared to claim the urn from his manager. Then something shocking happened. Bearer turned his back and refused to hand Undertaker the urn. Mankind caught up to The Undertaker and they continued to brawl. When Undertaker again tried to grab the urn, Bearer hit him with it, then gave it to Mankind for the victory. As Undertaker looked on in stunned silence, Mankind and Bearer left the ring together. Unfortunately for The Undertaker, the indignities had only just begun.

"I made The Undertaker what he was, but he lost his power, and now I will do for Mankind what I did for him," Bearer gloated.

However, within days, he and Jake Roberts, his former enemy, were wrestling in tag team matches against Mankind and Goldust.

The most dramatic encounter between Mankind and The Undertaker was in a buried-alive match at the In Your House XI pay-per-view

Determined be the victor of their 1996 feud, Mankind often used The Undertaker's casket and his urn, with its "magical" ashes, against him.

card on October 20, 1996. The objective of the match was as unusual as its name implies: to bury your opponent in a makeshift grave.

Morbid? Sure. Distasteful? Maybe. Too violent for words? No doubt about it. Memorable, too. The Undertaker won the match by burying Mankind, but he paid a price for victory. After the match, he was attacked by Bearer's newest protégé, a mysterious man called the Executioner who beat up The Undertaker, placed him in the grave, and, with the help of several other rulebreakers, filled it with dirt.

Yet, as we had seen in the past, stopping The Undertaker wasn't quite that easy. The final image for TV viewers that night was of The Undertaker's hand shooting up from the grave and through the dirt.

The Undertaker was set on revenge against the Executioner when they met at In Your House XII a month later. Mankind interfered and, along with Executioner, double-teamed Undertaker. The three men brawled back to the dressing room, leaving behind a path of destruction. Security guards had to place Mankind in a straitjacket while Undertaker chased Executioner outside, where he continued to batter his enemy.

Even when he wasn't wrestling Mankind or the Executioner, Undertaker couldn't avoid Bearer. At the 1997 Royal Rumble, interference by Bearer enabled Big Van Vader—a former WCW World champion—to pin Undertaker.

At times, it seemed as if The Undertaker had lost sight of his original goal, which was to win as many WWF World titles as possible. His count was stuck at one, and with no end in sight to his feud with Mankind and Bearer,

Undertaker hardly had time to make a run at the belt. He needed a major break to get his next title opportunity.

When WWF World champion Shawn Michaels had to give up the belt because of a knee injury, the WWF ordered a four-way elimination match in February 1997 to fill the vacancy. The combatants were Bret Hart, Steve Austin, Big Van Vader, and The Undertaker. According to the match rules, the only ways to eliminate an opponent were to pin him, force him to submit, or throw him over the top rope.

The Undertaker got off to a great start in the four-way match. He pummeled all three of his foes. Vader tried to hit him with a chair, but Undertaker retaliated and opened a cut near Vader's left eye. The four men brawled inside and outside the ring. Austin was eliminated first. Undertaker knocked Vader off the top rope. Only Hart and Undertaker remained in contention for the World title.

But neither Austin nor Vader had vacated the ringside area. Undertaker prepared to "tombstone" Hart, and Austin prevented him from doing so. As Austin and Undertaker fought, Hart clotheslined Undertaker over the top for the win.

Ironically, Hart lost the belt to Sid Vicious only one day later, setting off a critical chain of events.

First, WWF president Gorilla Monsoon announced the main event for WrestleMania XIII: Vicious would defend the World title against The Undertaker. The old WCW foes would meet again.

Second, concerned that Hart would beat Vicious for the belt, thereby depriving him of his

Sid Vicious (above) had the upper hand for much of his 21-minute title bout with The Undertaker, but when he turned his back on his challenger, The Undertaker grabbed him. After executing a tombstone pile-driver that kept Sid down for the count, The Undertaker won his second WWF World heavy-weight title on March 23, 1997.

title shot, Undertaker interfered in a Hart vs. Vicious match six days before WrestleMania XIII. Vicious retained the belt.

Finally, the day arrived: March 23, 1997. The WWF arrived at the Rosemont Horizon in Chicago for WrestleMania, its most important pay-per-view of the year.

Maybe the glare of the WrestleMania spotlight got to The Undertaker, because by no means did he wrestle the finest match of his career. He struggled for most of the 21 minutes that he was in the ring with Vicious, and rarely did it seem he had much chance at victory. There was little intensity as both men moved slowly and, seemingly, without intent. They exchanged bearhugs and headlocks. The crowd of 18,179 strained to keep its interest.

Vicious scored seven two-counts during the first eight minutes. The Undertaker dropped Vicious headfirst into the metal stairs leading to the ring, then delivered a spine-tingling powerbomb. Both men simultaneously scored with boots to the face and dropped to the mat with over 14 minutes expired.

Vicious got up and slammed Undertaker to the mat. Undertaker rocked Vicious with a clothesline. Vicious dumped Undertaker onto the arena floor and followed him out. Finally, Bret Hart made his entrance.

Hart grabbed a chair and attacked The Undertaker from behind. WWF officials escort-ed Hart back to the dressing room as Undertaker rammed Sid into the ringpost. Hart returned, refusing to stay away. Undertaker scored with a chokeslam for a two-count. Vicious turned his attention to Hart, and Undertaker sneaked up from behind.

Vicious had turned his back on the challenger. Seizing the opportunity, Undertaker connected with his tombstone piledriver, leaving Vicious slumped on the mat. Sensing victory, The Undertaker dropped on top of Vicious and waited for referee Dave Hebner.

The Undertaker had his second WWF World title. This time, he had done it without Bearer.

Never had the Rosemont Horizon been filled with so much noise! The fans embraced The Undertaker as if he were a hero.

"I am proud of being the new WWF champion," Undertaker said. "I have waited for this moment for a long time. The WWF is now entering a new era, a dark era, and I will take the WWF title where it has never gone before. Join me on my journey."

Unlike the past, when The Undertaker's journeys were wrought with fear and mystery, this one didn't seem so unpleasant to the WWF fans, who were more than willing to join him.

Soon The Undertaker would face a new threat. It was to come from his old friend and new enemy . . . none other than Paul Bearer.

6 BROTHER, CAN YOU SPARE A MATCH?

The threat had loomed since the breakup between Paul Bearer and The Undertaker. Nobody knew for sure whether Bearer really did have a secret or was bluffing. The Undertaker wasn't going to call his bluff.

"I know everything there is to know about The Undertaker," Bearer had said back in the fall of 1996. "Oh yes, I do! And do you think I will hesitate one little bit to use that knowledge to bury The Undertaker? Think again, small-minded fools. Think again!"

By June 1997, however, Bearer still hadn't revealed his secret. This much, however, was certain: The Undertaker had an idea what it was, and it had to have been a doozy.

After all, how else could Bearer have blackmailed The Undertaker into teaming with Mankind and Big Van Vader, two of his staunchest enemies, in six-man tag team matches?

"The Undertaker knows I can destroy his life just by revealing this secret," Bearer told *Pro Wrestling Illustrated Weekly*. "If he does not obey my every command, I will do it."

The plot got darker, deeper, and more sinister. The more Bearer threatened to reveal the secret, the more people wanted to know what it was.

In an attempt to topple his old protégé, manager Paul Bearer revealed to the world in 1997 that The Undertaker not only had an evil half-brother named Kane, but that Kane was alive and thirsting for revenge against his brother.

Indeed, this was the cruelest thing Bearer could have done. Just when The Undertaker was on top of the world as WWF World champion, Bearer was threatening to bring him down with one dirty utterance.

"He will do everything I say if he wants his secret to remain a mystery," Bearer further cautioned. "And as long as he listens to me, he'll remain WWF champion. If he loses that belt, I may just have to tell the world his secret."

The Undertaker held on to the belt. He had followed Bearer's orders.

Then the dastardly Bearer betrayed him anyway. In July 1997, he revealed the horrible secret. Undertaker's half-brother, whom he thought had died in a fire when they were both children, was still alive!

Although clearly shaken by the news, The Undertaker continued to wrestle. He pinned Vader, another of Bearer's charges, at the In Your House pay-per-view on July 6, 1997. He gallantly defended the belt against all challengers. But there was nothing he could do at SummerSlam '97 in his title defense against Bret Hart.

The match was a war. Several times the action spilled out of the ring as the combatants tried to pound each other into submission. With 24 minutes gone in the match, Hart clamped on his "sharpshooter" finisher, in which he uses his legs to tie up his opponent's legs, applying intense pressure to the lower back and thighs. The move always causes tremendous pain to the victim, but in this case, the pain was even greater: Hart had wrapped Undertaker's legs around the solid steel ringpost! Shawn Michaels, the wrestler who had been named special referee for the match, tried to break the hold. Undertaker kicked at Hart, inadvertently sending him into Michaels, who fell to the arena floor. Hart took advantage of the situation by slamming Undertaker with a chair. Michaels returned to the ring and asked Hart whether he had used the chair. They argued. Hart spat in Michaels' face. Michaels, enraged beyond words, swung the chair at Hart, who ducked. Michaels inadvertently struck The Undertaker across the face, flooring the big man and rendering him virtually unconscious. Hart went for the cover and Michaels, after hesitating briefly, made the three-count. The Undertaker had lost the title.

"What was I supposed to do?" Michaels said. "Maybe it was a mistake to allow the pin, but it was my fault that it happened. I let myself get carried away, and I shouldn't."

The Undertaker wasn't accepting Michaels's apology. He was incensed over losing the belt and vowed to get revenge, which came at the Ground Zero pay-per-view on September 7, 1997, when he tore into Michaels.

But there were other things on Undertaker's mind. Where was this long-lost half-brother? It didn't take long for him to find out.

The alleged half-brother was a wrestler named Kane, and his manager was Paul Bearer. Kane arrived in the WWF in September 1997, nearly the spitting image of The Undertaker. Kane was 6' 7" and 345 pounds, and he had long, reddish hair, ghoulish eyes, and alabaster skin. Nobody could see his face because he wore a mask. His body was a mass of solid muscle. He was mean. He was ferocious. And he was angry.

*Meeting his half-
brother in the
ring for the first
time, Kane seizes
the ringside steps
and prepares to
smash The Under-
taker during their
brutal match at
WrestleMania XIV
on March 29, 1998,
in Boston.*

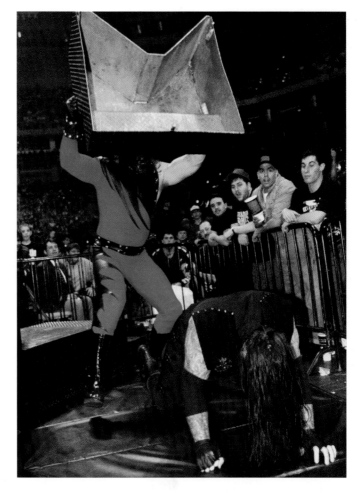

According to Kane, The Undertaker had left him for dead in a fire 20 years earlier. Kane had escaped, but the fire had left him disfigured and homeless. He was set on revenge, and he had arrived in the WWF to get it.

The Undertaker was shaken like never before. Never before had he backed down from a challenge, but he was reluctant to wrestle Kane, even when Kane interfered in Under-taker's "Hell in a Cell" cage match against Michaels.

Kane and Bearer kept up the pressure. Kane tore through the WWF ranks with frightening intensity, defeating one top contender after another by using what had been The Undertaker's trademark move: the tombstone piledriver. Bearer demanded matches against The Undertaker. Kane taunted his alleged half-brother. They searched for anything that would force The Undertaker to give in and grant Kane a match. The opportunity they were waiting for came up at the Royal Rumble in January 1998.

The Undertaker and Michaels were continuing their intense feud at the Rumble. The only way to win the match was to roll his opponent into a ringside casket and shut the lid. As Michaels mounted his offensive, Kane rushed down the runway, attacked Undertaker, and rolled him into the casket, giving Michaels the win.

The worst was yet to come. Kane and Bearer locked the casket and rolled it down the aisle. Kane grabbed an ax. Bearer picked up a can of kerosene. Kane chopped holes in the top of the casket and Bearer poured kerosene into the holes. Then, as the sellout crowd looked on in shock and horror, Bearer lit an entire pad of matches and set the casket ablaze!

The Undertaker somehow survived this horrific incident, but he didn't return to the ring until March. By then, his focus was clear: he cared only about hurting Kane.

Kane and The Undertaker met for the first time at WrestleMania XIV on March 29. The match was violent, brutal, and intense. Twice, Undertaker tombstoned Kane. Twice, Kane kicked out before the count of three. Once, Kane tombstoned Undertaker. Undertaker kicked out before the three-count. Seemingly, the only men in the world impervious to the tombstone were these two men.

The third tombstone, however, was the charm for The Undertaker. Kane couldn't kick out as Undertaker covered him for the pin and a well-deserved victory.

If The Undertaker thought the victory had settled matters with Kane, he quickly found out that he was mistaken. As soon as the match ended, Kane went after The Undertaker and tombstoned him onto a steel chair. Clearly, the match at WrestleMania was just the first battle in the war between these two giants.

So they wrestled a second time. Then a third time. And a fourth time. It got to the point where The Undertaker didn't wrestle anybody but Kane. Brother vs. brother was quickly getting stale to everybody but the brothers. Once so reluctant to fight Kane, Undertaker was now doing little else.

Around this time, something rather remarkable was happening in the WWF. Federation owner Vince McMahon Jr., in an attempt to boost the company's Monday night TV ratings, began taking the WWF in a new direction, emphasizing sports entertainment, rather than just plain sports. Wrestling, which had always had its sideshow aspects, was becoming more show than sport.

To further his agenda, McMahon became involved in what would become a heated feud with Steve Austin, who had won the World title from Shawn Michaels at WrestleMania XIV. Owner vs. wrestler became the hottest feud of 1998, and The Undertaker found himself right in the middle.

The entire situation was, to say the least, bizarre. Desperate to get the belt from around Austin's waist, McMahon signed Kane and Austin to a first-blood match at the King of the Ring pay-per-view on June 28, 1998. The winner would be the first person to make his opponent bleed. Somehow, McMahon also convinced Kane—without Bearer's consent—to announce to the world that he would set himself on fire if he failed to win the World title.

Not surprisingly, it didn't take long for the match to get out of hand. When referee Earl Hebner was knocked out after colliding with Austin, Mankind and The Undertaker both stormed the ring. As Austin held Mankind, The Undertaker, who had defeated Mankind earlier in the night in a "Hell in a Cell" match, prepared to whack him with a metal chair. But Mankind ducked and Undertaker struck Austin full in the face. The blow opened up a cut on Austin's forehead and when Hebner recovered and saw Austin bleeding, he declared Kane the winner and the new champion.

Bearer, who now claimed to be Kane's father, was ecstatic. "My boy! My boy!" he exclaimed after the match. "The WWF champion! I'm so proud of my son. It just goes to show the greatness that runs in the Bearer genes. You thought you were going to watch Kane burn, didn't you, Undertaker? Well, who's having the last laugh now?"

Indeed, who was having the last laugh? One night later, Austin regained the belt from Kane. Bearer was no longer laughing.

There was something extraordinarily odd about what had happened. Although Austin and The Undertaker combined to beat Kane and Mankind for the WWF World tag team championship on July 26, 1998, Austin was suspicious of his new partner. He wondered aloud whether Kane and Undertaker were conspiring to do him in, proclaiming, "Steve Austin doesn't trust anybody. What makes you think I need Undertaker's help to be a tag team champion?"

Austin and Undertaker had argued on the way to the ring before their tag team title victory. Once the match started, Undertaker had been reluctant to help Austin as he was being double-teamed by Mankind and Kane. When the match ended, there was no celebration. Undertaker

Vince McMahon Jr. sent The Undertaker and his half brother Kane after Austin in hopes of ending Stone Cold's reign as WWF champion.

walked back to the dressing room with both belts draped over his shoulder. Austin simply stared.

Indeed, Austin had no reason to trust The Undertaker, and The Undertaker had no reason to trust Austin. Nobody had any reason to trust McMahon. Still desperate to get the belt from Austin, McMahon demanded a series of triple-threat matches, in which Austin would have to defend the World title simultaneously against both The Undertaker and Kane. Little by little, Austin's suggestion that Kane and The Undertaker were in cahoots became more reasonable.

McMahon had tried for months to control both The Undertaker and Kane. He suggested that if The Undertaker won the World title from Austin at SummerSlam '98, Undertaker would "need Vince McMahon." But for what?

"Friend or foe?" McMahon asked Undertaker during the August 24 airing of *Raw Is War* on the USA TV network.

The Undertaker refused to answer. Equally alarmed was Bearer, who couldn't believe it when he saw Kane and The Undertaker walking to the ring side-by-side.

Bearer demanded that Kane destroy The Undertaker. Kane didn't move. Instead, he walked away as The Undertaker pounded on Bearer.

The main event of SummerSlam '98 at Madison Square Garden went off without a hitch. For seven minutes, Undertaker and Austin battled furiously. Then, to nobody's surprise, Kane walked out to the ring.

Austin suspected he was in big trouble. But rather than enlisting Kane's help, The Undertaker told him to return to the dressing room.

Kane followed his orders and never returned. Austin won the match, but there were more signs of trouble to come. Undertaker grabbed the belt and it looked as if the two wrestlers might come to blows. Undertaker, glaring hard at Austin, finally handed him the belt and walked back to the dressing room.

Kane reuniting with Undertaker was clearly against Bearer's wishes, but by that time, Kane had stopped following Bearer's orders. Kane and Mankind, who won the World tag team championship on July 13, 1998, had been scheduled to defend the belts against the New Age Outlaws at SummerSlam, but by then, Kane and Mankind were feuding. Kane refused to team with him. Bearer didn't attend the pay-per-view, but telephoned Kane in the hope of convincing him to wrestle. Undertaker intercepted the call and hung up.

In the aftermath of SummerSlam, McMahon turned up the pressure on Austin. He struck a deal with Undertaker and Kane in which they would battle Austin in triple-threat matches. McMahon made the stipulations clear: Kane and Undertaker couldn't beat each other.

"And if you touch me," McMahon told Austin, "Kane and The Undertaker will annihilate you."

Austin wasted no time testing McMahon's challenge. He struck the WWF boss, then was attacked by Kane and Undertaker. "Nothing personal," Undertaker told Austin. "It's just business."

Facing overwhelming odds, Austin held on valiantly for a long time, but he couldn't hold on to the belt forever. On September 27, 1998, in Hamilton, Ontario, Kane and The

Undertaker were declared cochampions after pinning Austin.

Kane and The Undertaker didn't know what to do. After all, how could two men hold one World heavyweight title?

They couldn't. The next night, the title was declared vacant. As part of McMahon's continuing plot to destroy Austin, Kane and The Undertaker wrestled for the vacant belt on October 18, 1998. In a devious turn, McMahon made Austin guest referee for the match and threatened to fire him if he didn't declare a winner.

Before the match started, The Undertaker patted Kane on the chest in a sportsman-like gesture. They shook hands. Austin emerged to a thunderous ovation. With 16 minutes gone in the match, Bearer came to the ring with a chair and told Kane to let him hit Austin. Kane turned away, and Bearer nailed Kane from behind. Undertaker grabbed the chair and hit Kane, then covered him for the pin. Austin refused to make the count. Undertaker confronted Austin, who told him to try again. When Undertaker turned his back, Austin kicked him and delivered a Stone Cold stunner.

Kane and Undertaker had played into Austin's hands. McMahon's plot had been foiled. With both men down, Austin made a three-count on both men.

WWF owner Vince McMahon Jr. got on Undertaker's bad side after using him in a bid to foil Steve Austin's championship. Striking back, The Undertaker assured McMahon he planned to take over the WWF.

"And the winner of the match," Austin declared, "is 'Stone Cold' Steve Austin!"

He wasn't. The WWF still had a World title vacancy. Austin was temporarily jobless after getting fired by McMahon, and The Undertaker entered a new period of his career during which he welcomed back Paul Bearer. The events of October 18 had convinced The Undertaker that he wanted his old manager back by his side. They also convinced The Undertaker that he no longer trusted Kane.

"You're stupid, you're weak, and you can't even speak for yourself," Bearer told Kane. "You never understood the dark side; therefore, I have no use for you."

The oddest thing about this turn of events was that in the 1998 version of the WWF, there were no longer such things as rulebreakers and fan favorites. Had Undertaker crossed the line back to rulebreaking? Would the fans hate him once again? Maybe. Maybe not. It all depended upon whom The Undertaker was wrestling. Against Austin? Rulebreaker. Against one of McMahon's men? Fan favorite.

Needing to name a new champion, the WWF held a 14-man tournament for the vacant belt at the Survivor Series pay-per-view on November 15, 1998. The Undertaker pinned Kane in the quarterfinals, but lost to Rocky Maivia in the semifinals when Kane interfered. Maivia eventually beat Mankind for the title.

Suddenly, it was as if the first six months of 1998 had never occurred. Once again, The Undertaker and Kane were battling several times a week. Bearer was as devious as ever, but the fans stayed squarely in Undertaker's corner because he was facing the most hated clique in the WWF: Vince McMahon's Corporate Team.

"The Undertaker is back by my side, and together we will conquer the WWF," Bearer crowed to *Pro Wrestling Illustrated* magazine after being chosen 1998's Manager of the Year. "Everyone, including Kane, had better watch out, for the reaper is coming. Oh, yes!"

Getting on The Undertaker's bad side may have been the worst move of McMahon's life. Over the following months, Undertaker has turned up the pressure on his boss. He has formed the Ministry, a group that includes the Acolytes, Midian, and Viscera. Their stated goal is to take control of the WWF. Don't bet against them.

Very little is certain in wrestling these days. After all, in what other sport can a man who relishes burying his opponents alive become so popular?

But it's usually a waste of time to try and figure out these things. After all, this is wrestling, and in wrestling, anything is possible.

Consider the man who had to borrow money to attend training school. He continued to pursue his dream, only to run into one roadblock after another. In 1990, one of the two major federations in the world decided it didn't want him.

Suddenly, he received his big break. The other major federation decided it had a plan for this man and would create one of the most unusual characters in wrestling history. The big question at the time was whether or not it could turn him into a star. Nine years later, we have the answer to that question. The man is a superstar. His name is The Undertaker.

Chronology

1965 Born Mark Callaway on March 24.

1988 Attends pro wrestling school.

1989 Makes his pro debut in the CWA.

Defeats Jerry Lawler for the USWA heavyweight title.

Makes his NWA debut as "Mean" Mark Callous.

1990 Makes his WWF debut as The Undertaker at the Survivor Series in Hartford, Connecticut.

1991 Takes on Paul Bearer as his manager.

Defeats Hulk Hogan at the Survivor Series for the WWF World heavyweight title.

Loses the WWF World title to Hulk Hogan at a rematch; the title is declared vacant.

1992 Attacks Jake "the Snake" Roberts and switches from rulebreaker to fan favorite.

1997 Defeats Sid Vicious at WrestleMania XIII for a second WWF World title.

Loses the WWF World title at SummerSlam to Bret Hart.

1998 Pins Kane in their first meeting at WrestleMania XIV.

With Steve Austin, wins WWF World tag team championship.

Teams with Kane to beat Steve Austin in a triple-threat match for the WWF World title; the title is declared vacant.

Further Reading

Ethier, Bryan. "The Kane Mutiny: Undertaker's Future Lies in His Past." *The Wrestler Digest* (Spring 1998): 89–91.

Ethier, Bryan. "Warning to Kane and Undertaker: Now That You're Together, Stay Apart!" *Inside Wrestling Digest* (Spring 1999): 44–49.

Ricciuti, Edward R. *Undertaker.* Woodbridge, Conn.: Blackbirch Press, 1994.

Rosenbaum, Dave. "Lighting a Fire Under The Undertaker: Stop Playing with Matches That Don't Matter." *Pro Wrestling Illustrated* (September 1998): 32–35.

"The Undertaker." *The Wrestling Analyst* (July 1998): 34–37.

Index

Photo Credits

All-Star Sports: p. 60; Associated Press/Wide World Photos: p. 50; Jeff Eisenberg Sports Photography: pp. 2, 6, 11, 12, 14, 16, 20, 22, 25, 28, 30, 35, 36, 38, 44, 54, 57; Sports Action: pp. 41, 46; WCW: pp. 8, 33.

DAN ROSS has spent the past 10 years observing and writing about professional wrestling. His writing on wrestling, basketball, and baseball has appeared in numerous publications around the world, and he is a frequent guest whenever European radio and television stations require an American viewpoint on wrestling. He lives in upstate New York with his wife, son, and dog, and likes to brag to neighbors about the wrestling ring in his basement.